Nuns, Nam & Henna

A Memoir in Poetry and Prose

Larry Berube

A PEACE CORPS WRITERS BOOK

Nuns, Nam & Henna: A Memoir in Poetry and Prose
A Peace Corps Writers Book
An Imprint of Peace Corps Worldwide

Cover photo: Author on guard duty for a medic detachment
treating village children in Cu Chi, Vietnam (1966).
All photos are from the author's collection unless otherwise noted.

Photo Credit: Page 8: Francois-Louis-Joseph Watteau, "The Death
of Montcalm" c. 1783. Gift of W.A. Mather, Montreal, 1953 under
copyright license agreement with The National Gallery of Canada,
Ottawa. Photo: NGC

To Sally

who I loved too late

Contents

Prologue

I used to live in an apartment in the French Hill section of Nashua, New Hampshire. My father took care of my three sisters and me while my mother worked as a waitress at the Modern Restaurant. She was very pretty.

One day when I was six years old my sister, Diane, and I were standing in the kitchen watching our mother at the kitchen table putting on lipstick while getting ready for work. My two other sisters, Linda and Jeanne, were asleep in their room.

All of a sudden, my father picks up a hammer and starts hitting our mother in the eye with it. My mother yells to Diane and me to go get help. But we just stay there frozen in place. She runs out to the porch screaming, "Norman, stop."

But my father keeps hitting her in the face as she bends backward into the railing. Finally, he stops and goes into his bedroom to lay down and cry. Our mother manages to come back into the kitchen and tells Diane and me, "Go to the store and call the police."

We go and tell the man at the store, "Our father is crying, and he hurt our mother."

After two policemen come, we go back to the

apartment. Our father is still on the bed crying and just lies there despite one of the policemen who keeps repeating, "Come on Norman, lets go."

Finally, he gets up and leaves while still crying. He is put in jail for attempted murder, and my mother is sent to the hospital for three months. Diane, Linda, and me are put in St. Peter's Orphanage in Manchester. Jeanne is too young for St. Peter's, so she is sent to St. Joseph's Orphanage in Nashua.

This is not my memory, but Diane's. It should be my remembrance because I'm the oldest by a year. But all I remember was standing there—paralyzed.

Years later, in my late teens, twenties, and thirties my mother would ask me, "Why didn't you go get help when I asked you to?"

This question would invariably come on holidays when she was in the kitchen cooking, and it would always be when she was drinking. My response was always the same. I would just stand there silently and still as I did that day long ago that tore our family apart.

That unanswerable question finally stopped about the time my mom and I (a black-out prone drinker) quit drinking for good. Thank God.

Part I: Nuns

My PTSD

I wake up screaming and look around. I'm not in my small bedroom but in a large room with a lot of beds in even rows filled with other boys. A large crucifix is on the front wall. The back wall has moving shadows that pass swiftly along like running ghosts which give me the creeps. Only later will I realize this crawl of light is only the reflection of headlights of cars driving by.

My nightmare is always the same. Jesus Christ is strapped to an electric chair and just when someone is ready to pull the switch—I wake up howling in a holy terror. After a few nights of this, the nuns put me in a room by myself because my screams are disturbing the other little boys' sleep.

The Orphanage

Screaming nightmares,
six years old
in a dormitory
with forty other boys.

Sentinels in ghostly uniforms
with hair hiding bonnets
armed with beads
and a silver cross.

The only sound
on their patrol
of the beds in rows
are rustling robes.

I learn to sleep
without my family
in my limbo
alone.

Nun Parable #1

The man didn't believe the hosts
given at Holy Communion were
the body and blood of Jesus Christ.
So one Sunday morning he went
to Mass and received Holy Communion,
but instead of swallowing the host,
he put it in his pocket and hurried home,
straight to the kitchen. He put the host
on the table and stabbed it with a knife.
Blood ran out of the host.

He ran from the house.

Francois-Louis-Joseph Watteau
"The Death of Montcalm" c. 1783.
Gift of W.A. Mather, Montreal, 1953.
The National Gallery of Canada, Ottawa.

Farewell

A curious calm comes over me
as I sit, ramrod straight on the hard
high-backed chair in the waiting room
and stare at the painting on the wall.

Later in life I will know it by its name,
The Death of Montcalm.
The general lies dying, surrounded
by his loving and devoted officers.

I'm waiting for my father.
I'm 6 years old
and resigned to staying here.
I can only hope for presents.

I ask for bananas and other fruits.
like some other boys get.
My father promises,
but I'll never see him again.

He leaves and
I am dry-eyed,
unlike the general's officers
on the Plains of Abraham.

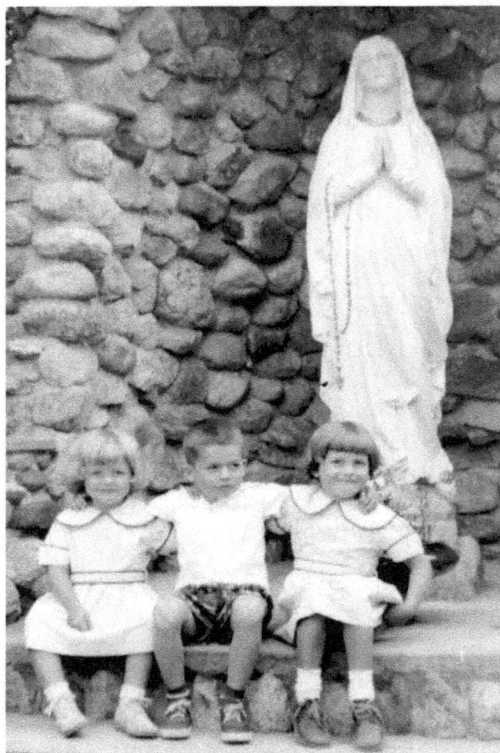

Left to right: Linda, myself, and Diane
by the grotto at St. Peter's Orphanage
in Manchester, New Hampshire

The Photo at the Grotto

It's Sunday, visitor's day
Meme and Aunt Laurance have come.

It's a special treat.
We're getting our picture taken.

Diane and Linda
are in matching dresses.

I'm the big brother
so I put my arms around them.

Meme asks us to smile
for a Brownie moment.

Holding the box camera
my godmother takes a snapshot.

In six years time
our only orphanage picture.

Time to Make the Toast

Sister Marie comes to wake me.
I'm in the third row,
fourth boy in.

Dutifully, I wake
and make my bed.
Hospital corners, of course.

It's quiet.
The new kid in the back row
has stopped crying.

Nuns are in the kitchen.
I smell oatmeal cooking.
I don't like oatmeal.

It's still dark outside
as I open packages of
Sunbeam Bread.

I place the slices in
the big turning toaster
that never stops.

The oatmeal is lumpy
and unlike Oliver
I don't want seconds.

Nun Parable #2

The boy was tired after walking all day. In the distance, high on a hill, he saw a castle. So he pushed on. When he got there, the big door opened, and a strange looking man invited him inside. The boy was scared, but he went in anyway because he was tired, cold, and hungry. The man served him a sumptuous feast in a great room that was heated by a fire in a large fireplace.

After eating, the man showed him to a bedroom, then left him alone. At the foot of a huge canopy bed was a pair of pajamas that he put on. Then he got between the sheets and felt the comforting weight of thick woolen blankets. He remembered that he hadn't said his prayers, so he got out of bed and started praying on his knees—the way good boys do. But before he finished making the Sign of the Cross, a large ax came down from the canopy and struck the middle of the bed where he had been lying.

He ran from the castle.

Waxing the Floors

On Saturday mornings we'd skate
with rags tied to our shoes
Side by side, across the floor.

The wax fumes filled our heads
but we soldiered on keeping our own cadence
arms flying, and out of step.

Our marching grounds began to shine,
but too many times, I fell in headlong plunges
until I was pulled from the ranks.

With a swooning head I'd watch
my comrades carry on
until the vapors claimed another boy.

On the girls side
my sisters, Diane and Linda,
marched on their own parade fields.

No jumps or spins allowed
just back and forth
with never a graceful turn.

Diane, like me, plowed forward
and skated straight and narrow.
But Linda went in all directions.

While hardly grounds for insubordination
she too was cashiered out.
Undisciplined—she was called.

The Laundry

Cheerful nuns folding cotton.
With silver crosses and gold rings,
married to the man in the sky.

Small and smiley, I come in.
Ordained, out of all the boys, to read
in French, *The Lives of Women Saints*.

On the outside,
beyond the tall fence,
Elvis sings *Jailhouse Rock*.

On the inside,
the sisters press their heavy habits.
And in my limbo

I read about the visions of St. Bernadette,
the humility and obedience of St. Gertrude,
and St. Theresa—The Little Flower of Jesus.

I read and read,
and after St. Joan of Arc saves France,
I leave with a lollypop.

Nun Parable #3

Scary noises
of wind and rain
wracking windows.
and racking nerves.

The nun tells us
we are hearing the cries
of cold and hungry
little girls and boys

who are screaming to get in
the orphanage, but they can't
because the nun says,
"There's no more room."

Saved

Hurricane Carol came quickly. All of a sudden, all the boys playing in the yard got caught in a slashing rain. The strong winds upturned the seesaws, and the swings clanged against their frames. We huddled and held on to the posts at the pavilion.

In the girls dormitory that overlooked the yard, the girls had been praying for safety from the storm. A nun, noticing our plight, lined up all the girls at the windows and had them pray for us. Because my sisters, Diane and Linda, knew I was down there, they prayed extra hard despite their sore knees on the hardwood floor.

Finally, during a lull, we boys ran inside. The nun told the girls, "The boys are saved because your prayers worked." The girls were happy, and fell asleep that night with smiles on their faces.

The following morning, the nun surveyed the damage. The boys play area was wrecked, but the girls play area was untouched. The nun turned to the girls, "See! That's because you prayed, and the boys played."

Saturday Night

On Saturday night, after ironing, cleaning floors and latrines, the girls took their weekly shower. They had to pass the boys' section on the way to the showers. A nun would march them by us in double file. Some of the boys would snicker at this weekly intrusion, while others just stared. On seeing me, the nun would tell my sisters, "Say hi to your brother."

We waved to each other.

Daddy Dreams

I dreamed I saw you, Daddy,
on a grubby Boston sidewalk.
You were taking slow sips,
from a crumpled paper bag.

A Red Sox cap, askew
shadowed your jaundiced face,
while you wiped your runny nose
with your dirty sleeve.

You saw me with your
sad, rheumy eyes
and held a shaky, bony hand out
palm up.

Why didn't you recognize me?
I have your eyes.
They call you homeless now;
you used to be a bum.

When you're covered with
cardboard on the Common
or sleeping on shelter sheets,
"Who do you dream of, Daddy?"

Part II: Nam

Tay Ninh City Bridge between the old French
compound and my favorite restaurant

Pass the Bat, Please

Hot, sticky, smelly.
I drink another Tiger beer
at my favorite restaurant near
the big rats of the winding river.

A pink plastic-sandaled waitress
walks the dirt floor around
discarded bones left for the dog.
I order steak and fries.

I see her in the kitchen as she
squats on the wooden counter.
She cuts my fries between
her bare feet.

My ARVN buddy brings me a package.
I see his offer:
A baked bat
with wings and head.

He passes it to me.
My widened eyes say no.
He grabs it by the wings
and bites the head off.

He crunches skull and bones.
Leaves nothing for the dog.
I finish the rest.
Tastes like chicken—gizzards.

Whorehouse #1

Monique walks by Wilkes and me while we drink a beer. I can't help but stare. Half-French and half-Vietnamese, she is the most beautiful woman in town. Wilkes notices my look and says, "Don't be *dinky dow*. Her boyfriend is a big bad Special Forces sergeant, and he'll kick your ass."

Later, I find a whore to spend the whole night with—a rare treat. I go to her place and stand my rifle in a corner. I take off green cotton. She takes off black silk. Afterwards, I awaken to her sister sliding into bed with us. *It's Monique.* I'm stunned and still as the gecko on the wall I stare at. Ten minutes later, the lizard moves a leg. I move an arm around Monique. She turns her back to me. I put my arm back around her sister and doze off. If not the sleep of the just, at least the sleep of a guy who won't get beat up.

Whorehouse #2

Wilkes and I are getting an attitude. We have to clean the little Vietnamese whorehouse in the boondocks.

It's monsoon season, and we need a dry place to greet the coming brass. So we sweep sticky condoms off the floor and out the door.

As the Huey touches down, the blast from the chopper's revolving blades shake the used rubbers in the puddles. The rain has stopped, so the visiting lieutenant decides to talk to us outside. The officer tells us we are doing a great job and helping to win the war, while he stands in a sea of spent skins.

Wilkes and I dare not look at each other for fear of busting out laughing.

Loading ammo

Humping Ammo

Me and Ski
riding shotgun
down Route One
on an ammo run.

Cu Chi to Saigon
joshing and joking,
having fun
on an ammo run.

Guarding the convoy,
from the Viet Cong,
with my M-14 gun
on an ammo run.

Loading 8 inch rounds
and sweating bullets
in the hot sun
on an ammo run.

Me and Ski,
with girls in black silk,
our work is done
on an ammo run.

Tay Ninh market along the
Von Co Dong River

Ants in my Pants

Gecko on the wall I see
at the house of Tee Wee.

But have no fear
Sarge and I are here.

We're not at a loss
with the smelly fish sauce.

But never have I read
of ants on the bread.

No, I never met
a black baguette.

I try to eat
but twist in my seat.

Instead
I pocket the bread.

Now I have ants
in my pants.

Bunker on perimeter of 25th Infantry
Division base camp at Cu Chi

On a Bunker

A whistling bullet passed my ear.
For me, who had not yet heard
a woman's cry.
It was too near.

For others, one score year
minus one or two,
a speeding bullet made no sound.
A woman's cry, did they hear?

The shades were loaned to me
at the local photo shop
in Tay Ninh City

Whorehouse #3

It was usually at night when Wilkes and
I would search for women. But one bright
day I thought, why not? Old Sarge said,
"Don't go. The VC will just use your
money to buy more guns and ammo."

But with minds set and rifles slung, we
headed out to a place we'd been before.
I knocked on the door in hopes of a whore.
But to our surprise, a skinny guy answered
and yelled a warning to his friends in back
who stumbled over chairs as they ran from
their secret meeting. We didn't shoot those
running Reds dead but walked away pretty
quickly ourselves because our only aim that
afternoon was to find a lay in the middle of
the day.

Vam Co Dong River at Tay Ninh City

The Little Rat

I wake and feel it on my chest,
crawling toward my face.
I yell and throw it off.

It waddles away, long tail trailing,
girth moving from side to side,
bigger than the fattest cat.

My sergeant wakes also,
"What's the matter?
Afraid of a little rat?"

Shook up, I look under
my green canvas cot.
The sand is covered with tracks.

They come for our pile of food:
fruits, veggies, and C-rations.
So why is it on me?

Now I sleep with a machete.
My salty sergeant has a .45
under his pillow.

At the old French compound
in Tay Ninh City

Vice and Advice

A Philippine medical unit moves in to the old French compound in Tay Ninh City where Sarge, Wilkes and I are setup. One of the Filipino soldiers becomes a drinking buddy of mine and starts worrying about me catching a disease. He's older than I am, a medic, and knows about things. So I listen. He advises me to smell a whore's vagina first, and if it smells like sour milk, I should walk away.

I don't know what to think or do because I had never been down close enough to it to get a good whiff. A few weeks later, I catch a dose of the clap.

A painful shot of penicillin cures the infection, but offers little redemption for a fallen Catholic boy.

Too many beers . . .

Close Combat

Against my temple he held a gun.
No, I didn't run,
that monsoon night in Nam
serving my Uncle Sam.

There was no thought of lead
entering my head,
for I had no cares,
thanks to too many beers.

It was almost friendly fire
for swinging at a silver-barred
Act of Congress
gentleman.

Part III: Henna

Arab Street

He jabbed the ass
of the ass
with an olive branch

and made a blood-trail
on the trail
while flies swarmed

over the back
and the mark
of the cross of Jesus.

Surveying in a small village in the Middle Atlas Mountain region of Morocco for a water project.

Henna Hands

At midday
in a land under the crescent
I escape the desert heat
in a cool mud brick hut
where I sit on a worn carpet
that covers the smooth dirt floor
and have my dusty hands
washed with rose water by my host
who serves me sweet mint tea,
the liquor of Arab hospitality,
and gets his humble reward
listening to my war stories.
A clay tagine dish is delivered
on the floor at the door
by henna hands.

Henna Feet

Later,
I view her in a worn veiled vestment
as she carries an old water jug
on her small crescent shaped shoulder
and leans her urn by the well
then shuffles off, hunched over in the
hot, dry sirocco blown dust
on henna feet.

Henna Hair

At twilight,
a lady friend of mine and Peace Corps volunteer
walks outside alone on her first day
in a small town she was placed in to teach
on a dusty plain surrounded by mountains that are
not majestic like the Rockies or the Alps
but more like the biblical mounts
of Abraham and Moses.

Unfortunately, her nearest male relative/escort
is 5,000 miles away, and when she returns
whore is written on her old wooden door
in beautiful, flowing Arabic calligraphy with its
elegant sweeping curves and loops.

Nevertheless, she stays, serves, and is befriended
by village women in cotton djellabas who pull
back their pointed hoods and put henna in her
hair and tattoo it on her hands and feet—gifting
her with luck and happiness as well as protection
against the darker forces of life.

Sally and the water man in Marrakesh

Sally

You never saw the crack behind my smile
while you poured your love into the colander
that was my heart.
The water man in the dusty street also smiled
but all you gave him were some coins.
How I wish my leaky heart
could have held as much as one of his tin cups.
Then I wouldn't be alone
with only a tourist photo
of that Marrakesh dude in a red sombrero
holding your hand.

Epilogue

TV Land

In the orphanage, I only watched TV on the occasional Sunday. And only if I was good and my name wasn't on *the list*. The nuns often told us, "Watching TV is a privilege and not a right."

After Mass and dinner, they would march us in single file to orderly rows of folding chairs. We sat quietly as church mice while the TV was on, *or else*. The movie I remember most was *Lassie Come Home*.

After six years in the orphanage, we went to live in an apartment with my mom. I was surprised she had such a huge TV. It was a 19-inch Philco, as big as the orphanage one. One Saturday morning, our cousin, Barbara, came to visit. My sister, Diane and I were lying in front of the TV with our elbows on the floor and our chins in our hands. Barbara sat on the couch behind us. All of a sudden, she started to yell at us, "What's the matter with you two anyway. That's a cartoon! You should be laughing." We turned around and looked at her like she was crazy then continued watching *Bugs Bunny*—silently.

Left to right: Linda, Diane and Jeanne.
Three-fourths of the Thanksgiving Day
Massacre wolf pack.

The Thanksgiving Day Massacre

We had a guest for Thanksgiving dinner. He was a boyfriend of one of my sisters, and we thought him worldly wise—he was from California. As soon as my mom took the turkey out of the oven and set it on the counter, my three sisters and I attacked it like a pack of wolves. We pulled all the golden, crispy skin off the bird and stuffed ourselves with it while our guest looked on in horror with bulging eyes and open mouth. He looked to our mother who just said, "I let them do it on this special day."

We were a dozen years removed from the orphanage where the nuns forced us to eat fast and finish everything on our plates, *or else*. Like when two nuns forced me to eat a salt pork sandwich they had made especially for me because after a baked bean dinner, I had left a bit of salt pork rind on my plate.

And the orphanage visiting room was also a distant memory, where we would gorge ourselves with homemade fudge and caramel given to us by our visiting aunt and grandmother because the nuns would confiscate it as soon as our relatives left, supposedly to pass it around to the other kids.

But we were young adults now and past the excusable teenage years.

Although our guest hadn't said a word, his mouth was still open as he watched with widened eyes the naked, massacred turkey being placed on the table between the mashed potatoes and cranberry sauce.

Inner Rain

In an icy puddle I lay
on this no blue in the sky day
feelings frozen like a fish fillet.

Down in the gutter I stay
far from the fray
keeping friends and lover at bay.

Will I ever get to slay
this muddled monsoon spray
of my blue and flowerless May?

The Reunion

Forty years for me,
cast on,
for others not so long.

We walked inside
the red brick place,
so small.

There was laughter
and tears.
It was our home.

For some of us,
not quick to smile,
a tortured grin.

On empty
our reunion we saw
with mirroring eyes.

Acknowledgments

I would like to thank the members of my first poetry group, Post's Unbound, in Nashua, New Hampshire. Especially, Lana Hechtman Ayers and Brent Allard, whose suggestions were always spot on and much appreciated,. It was a constructive critique workshop group, and that's what I most needed as a novice poet.

I am particularly grateful to Lorraine Lordi, who reviewed my poems and prose and provided insightful comments. She was my favorite writing professor at Rivier College, and made every student feel we were her own favorite.

My book is published under the Peace Corps Writers imprint, but is printed by CreateSpace which is a division of Amazon. Heartfelt thanks to Laura Annan for guidance through this publishing and printing process. Working with her was delightful and productive as she is smart, supportive and enthusiastic. Her knowledge of working with CreateSpace was invaluable in uploading my book and making decisions on layout and prepress services. She has been through this before and showed unfailing patience towards a first-time writer.

About the Author

Larry Berube was born in Nashua, New Hampshire. He has a B.A. in Writing and Communications from Rivier College. The poems in *Nuns, Nam, and Henna* are recollections from his boyhood experiences at St. Peter's Orphanage in Manchester, NH, his time as a young soldier in Vietnam, and as a Peace Corps volunteer in Morocco. He lives in Florida.
vetandpcvol@gmail.com